Outskirts

AKRON SERIES IN POETRY

Outskirts

poems by Heathen

 The University of Akron Press
Akron, Ohio

ISBN: 978-1-62922-151-9 (paper)
ISBN: 978-1-62922-152-6 (ePDF)
ISBN: 978-1-62922-153-3 (ePub)

A catalog record for this title is available from the Library of Congress.

∞ The paper used in this publication meets the minimum requirements of ANSI/NISO z39.48–1992 (Permanence of Paper).

Cover image: Detail from *Gloves* by Beverly Semmes. Courtesy of the artist and Shoshana Wayne Gallery, LA.
Cover design by Amy Freels.

Outskirts was designed and typeset in Garamond with Avenir titles by Amy Freels and printed on sixty-pound natural and bound by Bookmasters of Ashland, Ohio.

Produced in conjunction with the University of Akron Affordable Learning Initiative. More information is available at www.uakron.edu/affordablelearning/.

Contents

I have waited all my life for permission. I feel it growing in my breast. A war is storming and it is behind me and I am moving my forces into light.

—Eileen Myles, *Chelsea Girls*

For Jo

Uxor Pilate

I want no country, least of all

this one. Gather in the fields

on the outskirts of the village,

each of us a body turned to cloud,

signs, and wonders. Subtract us

from our birthplace, gape, opening:

O, birth pang and cry of origin,

thousands of waves on the face

of the lake. Where does a nation's

story end? Revenge,

a war horse reared back. O

I will kill my own countrymen;

I will kill my own kin. *Have nothing*

to do with that innocent man, Woman,

nameless, said. I saw it in a dream,

blood on all our hands.

Portrait of a Courtesan

Through the door of the surgery theater

I was bathed in light, ringed by blue-gowned hosts.

I cut off my breasts with a butcher knife.

Jesus said when they ask for your cloak give

your undergarments too.

                            Smell of baking bread

in ovens   sourdough starter that multiplies

and never ends   yeast and stars and stem cells

mother's milk on her blouse. Smile at the doctor

one last act of compliance.   In the morning

blood soaked the gauze, mortared it stiff.

Once there was a courtesan

and her name was Fillide Melandroni.

Caravaggio was her pimp.

Location: destroyed.

Look at us   girls made in our own image we

are the lost history of the world.

Demarcation Line

Dangling like phlegm from the horse's mouth

(same night as Bataclan)   the girl took her own life

(truth be told   men killed her)   who rules the world?

Soldiers' radios crackle to life her voice rings in my head

from one side of the border to the other   *mother*

what will happen if I die in a foreign land   child

you'll be buried among others   we would have done

anything   to change the way the story ended

and so every mother waits at every checkpoint

and every crossing   to carry your body safely home

Fuse

Let me tell you in that time in America, the children grew up

knowing survival like the back of their hands   girl

so thin SpaghettiOs out of the can and cold corn and peas

                                              clit

like a piece of bubblegum between the boy's teeth

not even all his grown ones in his gums yet

Pick and choose what scripture is truth and what's so useless

it's not even lies   hymns in four-part harmony   now forgotten

tales told in horror   the missing girl, thrown

to be eaten by hogs in their crowded lots

        Go back into America's new broke earth

all of us luminous in our nightgowns wandering through the unfinished

developments and subdivisions   the fields

where we learned to play war   and got so good at it

How did we get here so fast?   Arrived in the new century

explosives padlocked to our chests   crossing through the gate—

defense contracts and security clearances our inheritance

all of it redacted   an apple fallen into our opened chawing hearts

the clock ticks down   no time

left to unlatch the lock   girl with kerosene in her mouth

to numb a pain more powerful than your peace

———————————▶

She strikes the match   her only remaining light

Take your two cupped hands   cradle the small flame

she lit inside of you, (she needs your breath)

                                  and blow   blow

I Want to Tell You About a Girl, Captures

We came to watch celestial bodies fall, so far

from our own, our heads upturned in awe,

comets like eyestrings across your cornea.

We followed the trail by Spade Mill Pool,

marsh marigold and sallow in the bogs,

primrose and wild narcissus on the banks

near the black water reflecting the stars,

and wild anemone in the shady places.

Even in night's darkest, there are gradations

of dark. Boy from town, a soldier on leave

from the Troubles, says bodies are sunk low

down in the mud. Things he'd seen. Things

he'd had to do. I tell you, write this down

in your notebook: *Curiosity is insubordination*

in its purest form and kiss, muddy fingers

fondling each other's teeth, a form of *braucherai,*

old, old magic in the body, black pact.

Like pulling the heat from a bruise, it may be

that words are unspoken but the thing desired

be strongly thought. We are each a holy book stolen

and smuggled into life. And yeah, I'm calling you out,

every one, boys who hid the bodies, girls who promised

never to tell. Read the tales of ourselves and retell them,

no end to the possibilities. They joyfully hurl themselves

against the walls of their dying father's house,

His death, a blast hole for a door they walk right through.

Excerpt of a Letter from the Front Line: Black Bread

I buried my childhood self in the field, dropped

my garments under a wooden pallet, underwear

stained with blood. Forgive God his violence,

like a child. Waves crash in the cove of the Black Sea,

hapless like that, doomed, outcast from the grove, all

the apple trees cut down in wave upon wave of terror.

After Odessa, cursed with a single shot on the steps

of Potemkin sprawled on the asphalt, looking up at *what*?

Mouth opened in an *O* painted black, cracked spectacles

dangling from our ears   mercury pooling under the back

of all our heads.   During the ceasefire I called your name.

I can't explain *why* and anyway, isn't that a question

a child asks right on the cusp of loss? Next, memorizing

the names of guns and tanks, year, make, and model.

On the front line we ate black bread stained with cuttlefish ink

and I couldn't wait to tell you how it faintly faintly smelled like the sea.

Joan, Director's Notes

When the girl dies in martyr stories   her head goes on singing or testifies

Silence is all we get from the dead in this century   or a ghost
on the screen animated ⇸ by hand ⇸ in technicolor ⇸ segmentation
↓
 geodesic distance ⇸ Joan the Woman ⇸ red and yellow of flames
                                                    ↓
                                          heightening the dramatic effect.

My daughter lights a candle to the Saint in Notre Dame,
her first act of prayer. There were times, I confess
I wanted to be a martyr (also shahid, partizanka, terrorist).

Almost like believing out of spite.

A year later and Notre Dame is burning.

Do you see how there is always more to this story?

Who will get the last word?

And it's hard to know what century it is even until finally it dawns on us,

it doesn't matter in the least.   I do and do not believe this to be true.

Here we are still bound in this world's sob and heave

kissing the horses on the mouth

Photograph from the End of the World, Calanques

How beautiful you were, hair shimmering like fish scales

by the Mediterranean in the place where Mary Magdalene

hid in a cave and we camped that summer. Your brother cried

when he caught a rockfish blood and saliva dripping

from its sucking mouth   and your stepfather called him a pussy.

And now where has your brother gone? Diving from the heights

of the limestone cliffs into the cold sea, always the show-off,

disappearing forever. Waves crashed into the jagged rocks, disappeared

into themselves but kept reappearing like the azalea of sex opening

and closing its bloom between your legs. For a long time the moment

felt like a door on the hinge of the world

and without it the water would pour up into the sky   Genesis undone

the final FINAL deluge   just like all God's broken promises

swears he means it this time

it was you I saw when I can still see you like a trick of the camera, it was you who threw the fish back into the waters

and said NO whether by *water or fire,*   NO

I am not afraid of the world's end

Suffocation in Filadelfia, a Brief History of Moral Exceptions

Mennonite Colony, Paraguay

Two armadillos cut open, guts drained, their armored bodies

dangle from a telephone pole on the side of the road at the entrance to the colony.

The barn heaves with late afternoon heat.

A girl in the barn dreams of being strangled RIGHT NOW.

Talk among the women in a circle of plastic chairs

beside the blooming jacaranda, as they stripped the green pods in their hands,

and kidney-shaped beans pattered in the bucket, plunk, plunk, plunk.

She heard the talk between clop of horses' hooves,

and the clock on the mantle, which didn't tick. This *man* climbed

through the open windows of women and girls sleeping

and none would tell the men, no one to help if told. Some things

you swallow whole and bear in this world like the wad of cum

from your boyfriend and no matter who you are this has got to be kept

secret, straw sticking to your lips, between his stiff legs. Matter of life

and death. The boys hold their breath under the sheets, self-asphyxiating

as they jerk off, breaths of ragged wheat rustling between their gums,

Father's shirts starched by the girls for Sunday morning with horse semen.

Everyone is still wandering in the wilderness. There's this thrill of pain,

from the word *thirl* meaning pierce or bone—   which is it   to *give*

or *receive*? Who's on the bottom, all that mattered really.

Back in Ukraine, women were raped so often they died off, no more

helpmeets. In those days the men formed self-defense units, Christ

be damned. You can't be too sure what you'll do when the time comes.

History has a way of changing your mind, when you're in the middle of it.

Pogroms come from every direction, starvation and at some breath hold

break point you will fail. Women already knew this what the men

thought was a sudden dispensation, flailing indulgence only used   *in extremis*

women's bodies, all history, migration, and broken lands.   Do not

conform anymore to the pattern of this world do not conform

to the pattern of this world *Terror Praesentis*

they wept in one body   stuffing their babies' throats with sand.

Postcards from Miss World and the Angry Brigade

Four in the morning in the Schwenkfelder Church yard
the stars ripple and lilt, slits of light.

Before I existed my people practiced magic
they called Amish powwow, spells cast on scraps of paper
in the shape of stars

   Himmelsbrief
[[[Heaven's Letter]]]

folded and pressed into the palm of a hand.

I know I carry this knowledge in me,
                      their texts in my blood.

*

When I was young I was so afraid of demons, *ferhext.*
It took me a long time to grow up and learn how to be afraid and still love.

In London I saw a photograph of Francis Bacon in a beaded flapper dress,
Eton crop in his clenched fist.

                The caption said his father

had him horsewhipped by the groom when the artist
                      was just a boy.

*

I was so angry.

A bomb went off behind the BBC van in front of the pageant

The air rang out in its socket of silence   all balance lost,

a mess the body makes.
What I want to know.   Which head gets the crown?

Magnetic Girl

I was a wonder   propelling mountains like carp
into the sea   no match for me   all men trembled

just ask the Baptist minister how I hurled the professor
and the physician
                              jumping jacks around the room

The General's homing pigeons quivered
necks broken, all those commands,
shredded to confetti.

The audience flocked and cheered for me!

The men the men in twos and threes
burly and stocked   braced their stance   tensed

their muscles against a pole pressed
to my dainty hand   fulcrum and lever

invisible   redirecting the force until they staggered

Now the electrical storm floats on the horizon
and I just sit back and watch it pass

I quit the shows   that life   of great feats

Nothing much to it   a shrug
of the shoulder   sleight of hand   But how

they all believed, wanting to believe
the ideomotor effect.   Lay your neck in my lap

Lay your neck in my lap   I'll turn into you and

turn you into me.

Eye Teeth, Restraining Order

Deal, Kent, England, 1989

The brake fern is in leaf. One last walk
in the woods on the way to the dance
at the armory. She saw a few hare, finch,
nettle creepers, and lapwings. She swam here
with the boys that summer, Baron's ponds,
dozing in the grass, reading *Cream* magazine.
All those naked boys in their jacked-up courage.
Morse code of tapping rain. She wanted to belong.
I mean I. I was calling the tawny owls. You said,
just moan or cry out and they come. Saturday night,
a hardcore band and I was knocked out, combat boot
of a boy in a stage dive to my head. Dust of history
on my cheek, a bomb went off   at the Deal barracks
nails   flew through the walls   two people dead.
When I came to, you were dragging me by my ankles,
the way my brother once roped the calf in Wyoming,
his delicate fingers pressed against its neck. O how
all your bodies troubled me, troubled. A lampshade
of flesh between us, shadow puppet on a screen. I see
you under the spotlights, singing in a photograph,
on a stage, mouth frozen mid-scream. I'm not allowed
to hear you. I'm not worshipping you. I'm searching
for the soft spot I can sink my teeth into.

Instruction Manual, Baltic

I'll hamstring you
cut your tendons

(these are the things I know)

sensory flight instruments of insects
whirring in the summer heat
above scythed fields

Her eyes, hepatic-dark

orchids with their barbed hooks

Rain in its orneriness
child's play of war

smell of oil tar from the furnaces
drifts through the forests.

Little teeth of pinion,
gears of language
spinning in your mouth

pink root nux vomica

I've got all the curses
all the healing balms

deep cry of a wild animal is her call

O the arrogance of endings
and the men who try to write them

Here is the Saaremaa yellow rattle
in wet meadows and spring fens

rare, very rare and it hides itself in nature

a soldier's helmet half-buried
in the peat and saxifrage,
its painted red star brilliant
as mercury in the mud

This island, providence of women
and a thousand overlooked creatures

pen this psalter   open your book to me

I will open my book to you

Iftar (with the Stooges), Sarajevo

For Edin

Light of the lamps on the red geraniums, we leaned
from the balcony into the night's air dense with ghosts,
stretched far out over the railing, as if we might bridge
this world and that, our fingers in the air trace the faint
outlines of graves in the settled ground. In our longing
to reach them, to make out their residual forms, our bodies
were touching (are still touching now). See there, in the dirt
the only safe place from snipers, where the hastily dead
were hastily buried. Five years since the war's end, iftar
again, bullet holes in the mantel of the door and down the hall.
Never fill them in, we promise. Rain fell over our hair, faces,
into the garden at peace, a peace both ordinary and miraculous
even so and even so, I still half-collapsed at the cannon blast.
Vulliamy said, *The war is dead, long live the war!* What is the name
of the song drifting that night from the bedroom, drifting still?
You asked and I couldn't remember, or who it was singing:
Your pretty face is going to hell because after the war, neither
one of us could remember, even things we knew by heart.
Maybe if you asked me now after so much history was written
down, I would speak the truth out loud, in an instant of reckoning,
shout, *Man in Instant Death*! *by Capa!* After all, history reveals
the truth of ourselves in action, doesn't it? I swear I would know
the answers to every question and I would call out to strangers,
I have something to tell you! But I was wrong. That is not
the correct name of the photograph in question. It's called
The Falling Soldier and some say it was staged. Also,
the man shot was an enemy combatant, hardly worth the pathos.
I don't understand anything at all, even after all the books
I've read on the subject. I still lap doglike at the viscera
of what lies between us, shell blasts like bear claws,
where the water pools in the sidewalk. It's not prayers I say
so much as *Tell me the truth*. I cannot conceive of a harder fast
than all the missing so long gone. I'm hungry. All I want is to eat.

Abide

She clopped herself in the face   like a quickening inside
that's what his mother told him about how she knew
him in her womb before he was known   *Unstable*

is what he heard said of HER   later in life, from uncles,
cousins, something about it sounded like confession.

                               Tracks shift and bend,
looking for ballast   She said, *You need a Bangalore*
torpedo to cut barbed wire and detonate buried mines
that's the kind of stuff she knew, *had* to tell him useless shit
C'mon! You have to bang away at it!   He always wanted
to please her

                  Out on the range, the grasses dried to tinder
coarse hair from the bodies of elk snagged on the razors
and the wind pushed its labor against your whole body,
                                    you alone, only
resistance for miles around   and the cows trailing blood
and fetuses

                  Never saw a woman like that, so tough. Good
luck, kid. She once tried to put a spell on herself to shut up
her own mouth, if only she'd never say anything to hurt him
but it backfired, and because she couldn't talk, she hit him.

He told her at last, Mama, I'm not the man you think I am. She said,
I never thought you were anything but the thoroughfare of God.

Kill Yr Idols, Liner Notes

Just three notes is all you need, and an amp,
said Thurston behind his sunglasses, he swears
he wears indoors not because it's cool
but for his failing vision, and he can't figure out
the tabs on the computer screen so he asks for help. Come here,

don't be shy. I've said it all before, broken record,
a compulsion   to sing the same song

what was that noise   that skip
in the beginning? *Jack HeyJack*. Look, Patti's in the kiddie pool

now. He shows the slide of *her*   LOOK AT HER

                                        projected on the classroom wall,
panties half off,   he doesn't see
                        me, my finger in her wound, styptic.

Oh, I make him uncomfortable.
I tell him I was raped; class goes silent.

It's about *respect*, the distance between stage and audience, he says.
I said very quietly like a tiny mouse *fuck you*.

Once I read in *National Geographic* about this naked mole rat with fangs
that lived in the Arctic and had a heater in its head to burrow tunnels in the
ice and you had to be careful if you lived up there because they would erupt
from their tunnels and eat your face sometimes.

I was amazed and astounded and told everyone I knew before I realized it
was April Fool's.

On the last day, I ran to the mic and interrupted Thurston on the panel
because I was PISSED.
But you know what I said? *I'm sorry... I'm so sorry*
and then I told him off.

The audience clapped but I thought I saw Eileen Myles roll their eyes,
disgusted at my apology.

I'm sorry, Eileen. I tried my hardest. I'll keep trying. I'll do better next time.

He says we should take a break, get some fresh air.

        Check this out,   Can you do that? Arrest

the bleeding? It's my secret knowledge. I've got so many tricks.

I've got it all in this book

I say, pounding my chest.   The storm pops its strings

and heartthrob,
                you are the last act so please
come back inside and teach me something I don't know already

Hey, is this a true story?

Question: do you reap with a sickle or a scythe?

I have to remind myself what I came here for,
NOT to seduce. NOT to KILL YOU.
Six of one, half dozen of the other.

What'd you do, baby girl? What'd you do?!   Sliced off his head, mama
left it in the driving wheel
and ran away.

She lives in the pines, in the pines.

She's got nothing more to say to any of you.

Assassin in the Gallery, a Written and Signed Confession

The gunman in his tight-fitting suit, legs spread
the glamorous stance, arms outstretched in eternal aim   cock of the gun,
WHY IS HE SO BEAUTIFUL TO ME?

 He stands over the dead man beside the paintings

HERE I AM, I cry out, begging him to LOOK AT ME, vector clock in my fist,
          —an ordering out of chaos? Fat chance.

Infection is more like it, some bad feverish obsession.

I can't help myself, curled at the base of the toilet.

My breviary is your breath and voice I go back to
playing it on a loop in my head   notes that tremor

over your vocal cords   your singing soothes me

I don't have to speak   your breath between the melody,

so quick, the intake steadies my breath. Two men are alive

in this gallery—one a murderer, the other a stranger

with a kind countenance. Who should have to pay the price?

My life strikes its teeth against the rock   strikes its fist

against the water   demands your attention   Look,

one of us is going to have to die, besides the dead man

lying there like an actor on a stage, except he's nobody.

We have already forgotten his name.   Snow falls

on his black coat, blood pooling under his head in the shape
of another man.

At the Crossing, a Warning Signal

On the cusp of the mountain a hawk watches the fields. To repent
is to turn in a different direction.

You may find there a checkpoint
and nothing at all to drink.

O what a multitude they were, these children   hum of multitudes

The lake is ringed with landmines and patrolled by men
and there's a truck roaring over the gravel road with the sound of mountain wind,

ash like human dust floats and sparks,

little gas lamps of the houses hiss, rays bending in concentric rings.

A worker found a body of a woman trying to cross
down in the river, hooked on a bulwark.

Was he the intercessor?

The HRD dogs showed no sign of interest,

as if even her scent was lost. The man who found her wept.
You can still hear him weeping. But don't be fooled.

It's not for you no   It's not for you.

Bail Bond

Take me down to east Texas in your car, blue vinyl seats
and the windows rolled down, a raid of locusts swarm

each one closing its tempest of wings over my mouth.
I turn to look at you from the passenger seat and you slap me,

every time. I turn my head to look at you, again and again,
a compulsion, thorax shivering between my teeth

and you slap it out. I *know* you, I clap back and I swear
my favorite fella, you are already dead.

I wanted to sleep in hot motel rooms, collect rare minerals,
dance the two-step for joy with you, but fuck-all you couldn't

keep up. You think I don't mean what I say? Answer me
when I ask. What did it feel like? Like love in a boarded-up town?

Like fucking at the end of the road, when you said, *Scream,*
I said scream. You know, you could write a murder ballad about it,

but you'll be too dead.

*

Come on, sister, let's coax them all into the grove on the outskirts,
quicksand or sinkhole, some kind of trap. Low murmur of tractors

binding them in the red dirt, gust of hot air and your hair's a mess
with all that blood in it. I know full well what we did *terror cimbricus*

and it felt so right to see them run for it. Here in this new country
we've born, you've got some time to kill and you're not even guilty.

C. D. said, it's *Cooling Time*. Sister, it's our time for cooling time,
get back up off your knees and just carry me off to your bed, drop me
on the hotel sheets, finger me like truing an instrument,

like you and me alone can fix it.

The Hearing, Sarajevo

I once believed you caught a bird in your hands
                     as if what was happening in me was love.

It was a photograph, a red cardinal cradled in your palms
and I believed it so fully,   the moment of believing it,   a gasp,

intake of breath,   the way I'm willing to believe
everything unaccountable.   You told me it was stunned

against the window is all,   and you'd gone and picked it up,
not caught it,   but three years later I still believed

it flew into your hands,   as easily as I did,   or tried to do
stunning myself like that,   and you refused to pick me up.

I'm waiting at the bus stop in Sarajevo,   still believing.

Sparrows flutter around my feet so close I can make out each
individual feather   hewed to the breast

like the ninety-nine names of God
                          written on the dome of the mosque.

Won't you hold one small beast
of me in your palm   not a question?

                         but a prescription. For loving me back?

Ear bent down to the bird of my mouth when I ask.

What does it say about what kind of love it is
                         that I believed you caught a bird mid-

flight and it settled into the nest of your fingers,

effortless! Both the trick and the belief in it.

*

Nameless birds against clouds now
         behind the stone walls of the madrassa,

in the ancient room where travelers
         were always welcomed in and given shelter,

find me in the hole in the dirt beneath the flagstones
where the Haggadah was hidden, buried during the wars.

Daisy-cutter bombs, burn bags, hellhounds, so much spectacle

  guest is God   waiting,

*

I once loved what would outlast pain
         but you are like these birds who come and go
in my dreams;
          with whom I have no language to share.

The adhan is calling now,
his voice telling a story that never ends.

I hope you can hear me from here.

In the First Hour of the War We Didn't Believe There Would Be a War

Caesura of breath when she saw him slumped
over the circuitry of downed power lines,
water pooling around his mouth.

Reboant, resounding, reverberation of the armies
gathering over the hill. *Trying to find the etymology
of God's name, something seems out of joint.*

Pain clusters its mine field around my heart,
like a throbbing in the eardrum after the soldier's first shout.

Sequins of the dead in the clouds.

—a child dead in the riverbank, already just a fragment.
We have all now become vagrants in this city.

Live as if you're already dead, said the dead man.

El Call

In the alleys of the Jewish Quarter on the wall
of the era, you can find Hebrew inscribed on a stone,
taken from the cemetery by the emperor's decree.

It was meant to be ordinary, neither cornerstone,
keystone, nor cap. One solitary stone among others.

Now pilgrims walk across the city just to touch it,
fingers grazing the scripture: *Its light burns evermore.*

Above my head the parakeets call my name in feathers
like tongues of fire above the alleys of the dead. God
sends birds to reclaim the song of what we once erased,

calling memory from the stone: merciless, merciless.

Cloud of Witnesses

Look how sheepish the man's rage is,

how it tucks into a smile over his clenched teeth

his pluck hands like plump sorrow around any girl's throat.

*

But I remember *your* voice, so different,
extravagance I have to stop up my ears against
or I will collapse.

*

The stars of trillium, apprehensively unfurling
as slow as an afternoon. My head at rest against
your vulva.

*

When the men in congregation

start shouting, I cover my ears again:

Shut up shut up, you're not even here
you're in Dubrovnik!

*

the blood of me leaks from your gums

My body floats in your mouth
like duckweed on the pond

Molotov's Announcement

After Vasily Grossman, A Writer At War

All eyes turned up to the voice above their heads. Church
spire at the end of the street and a man's balled fist pressed
against the back of the woman's arm. He just wanted to touch
her, even in that moment of terror, he wanted to touch. Sirens
smell of perfume from the hit pharmacy. The thing about history
is that once it catches you, what you once believed is gone
in an instant. Like the portrait of the man in instant death,
too many details to absorb in the action unfolding before your eyes.
In a sea of violence you live by taking it in, exhale, inhale, exhale
and there is nothing but witness, no analysis, no moral or *finis*
at the end of the film. You cannot give a sermon, make a rebuttal;
    there is no treatise. All of these things exist outside of the world.
Here there are only boletus mushrooms and a city burning
in the eyes of a horse lying on its side in the street. The spire
has fallen in on itself. The man has pressed his fist through
the empty air where the woman stood only seconds before. He
stumbles at her disappearance. He feels as if he'd heard a fable
and it's on the tip of his tongue, something about God, the sensation
proof that he loved her. It's extraordinary. Extraordinary, he mouths.

Map to the Field of Palaces

A river of bats flows from beneath the overpass and lifts into the sky.
                              I saw this with my own eyes and saw no end
to its current, a transfer of energy out of the shadows below
into vast night and in the blackness
                              heard their wingbeats,
like water over stones.

In the refugee camp, the children taught me
how to turn the cigarette labels inside out
and sometimes you would find a surprise,
a comic strip or coupon for bubblegum.
Did we forget we even had a body?

Curiosity is the only honest way to live, said Miljenko.

A child at the edge of the camp wanders through the shell fields,
                              in a labyrinth of stacked spent mortar casings,
like wandering through the great halls of the zodiac.

He calls his mother, his voice echoing through the hollow metal tubes.
Someone stove in her head. From *stave,*
from *staff,* from *spare not the rod.* A long history of harm

in language. Someone who was an enemy and has now
disappeared, has disappeared his mother, *escaped* thinks the boy,
though he can't imagine
what justice he might do, no language for justice in a child.
Only a call, a wild cry.

Out in the fields beyond barbed wire the whole city heard of this miracle
from *The Unwomanly Face of War.* How between snipers on the front lines,
a beautiful horse appeared, her mane and tail blowing in the wind, snowflakes
gathering on her eyelashes. Everyone held their fire. No one wanted to shoot,

just watched her, eating grass through the shallow snow, melting under her
    breath,
the shoots still green under her warm tongue. She stopped the war once and
    for all.
Never did the war continue the same way again. Mars flickered dim into a dust
    mote
in the soldier's eye, blotted out by the back of his hand, again and again.

Back at camp, the rumble of mortar fire never ends.
But the war is done, the war
no longer exists, just an endless river of pain throbbing,
like the pain of a tooth dulled with a mouthful of kerosene.

Every day brings some uncanny, unexpected discovery of direction,
a showerhead found half-buried in the woods. The secret language
between us connects us to home and God at once: a gold tooth
embedded in the pine. The pelican feeding her young with blood
she pecks from her own chest. We never cease our wonder.

Bewilder: *to lose in pathless places, to confound for want of a plain road,*
from wilder, meaning to lose one's way, as in a wild or unknown place.
When I walk with you in the country between us, I am never lost.
And I mean this sincerely, though don't call me sentimental.
I am always, always so full of violence.

Compass, compassion, compatriot, my true love, won't you please
walk beside me? Walk within me? Elizabeth Bishop said,
without regard for peril. Put your fingers in my wound.

Here I am;
accompany me.

The Fog

For Amila

The city was veiled: battlements of brutalist apartments
still scarred by mortar rounds from twenty years ago seemed

to levitate, an aversion to the solid earth, its illusions. Why
cover the scars when everyone knows war will return, no use

pretending. Clouds hung heavy with diesel exhaust and coal
smoke, so thick the taxis stopped running. Across the street

from the CNN affiliate was a building in ruins, one out of many
in this city we love,

and it seemed—why is it that everything *seems* here?—

seems to be still smoking from the siege,
but it was only a campfire and the homeless slept

within that *seeming*, within the house of their seeming selves,
in a ring of shadows. We were not at that moment afraid of men,

but of the packs of dogs following us through the blackened snow,
snouts low to the smell of hunger and bone, moving like one beast

through mountains of trash and the promise of hot broth in the cups
of strangers. I love you, *sister*. I love you, *brother*.

We called them wolves, and they veered away from us in mercy.

Cut Your Engines and Cool Your Wings

My stepfather visited me in a dream
and he looked like Elvis. I asked him
how it was he had risen from the dead,
and he said my question was very rude.

He died a month before my dream of him,
and I had refused to come to his deathbed,
even though my brother said he wanted me
to come, and he was sorry for what he'd done.

I emailed my brother back, subject line:
HE SAID I HAD A TIGHT LITTLE ASS!
referring to the time I was eleven. My brother
without skipping a beat said, *But he's crying and*

I have found a little kindness can go a long way.

In my dream I said to my stepdad, *Wow,*
you're like Lazarus! And his resistance crumbled
and he seemed shy and a little proud.

I woke up that bright morning in Barcelona
and felt ashamed, as if I had been found out.
As if the dead were calling me to repent
for sins I have not committed.

I walked out onto the balcony, air a cloud
of birdsong, wild parakeets dizzy
with grief, leaning so far across the precipice
I might fall
down to the scaffolding platform below

where a workman's yellow hat and reflective vest
were dropped in a heap like graveclothes folded in light.

Laying on of Hands

Her body, cocked under the catalpa trees,
hips & strap-on jut against the wet grass

of her sex. Thrust of cicadas against the flesh
of black locust leaves and racemes of flowers,

loose clumps of honey musk droop
above their heads and spread legs.

The Franciscans believed this was the tree
that kept St. John alive in the wilderness,

but they were in the wrong territory of *false*,
so it was left out of the canon. I believe

in every new interpretation, all the possibilities
of lust. Black Sabbath on the pickup truck radio.

Summer's wasps hushing at the lips of open cans
of Milwaukee's Best, stingers crystallized with sugar.

Cadence of locusts in the timber
and labored breath of the night pressing its palms

over our collective colonialist mouths,
but these two lovers are unruly and you cannot stop

their hunger. Larry Levis said, *What holds the word*
to the thing it signifies is desire

the girls' flames of tongues:
Enlarged by grief and their refusal to vanish.

Wild Orchid

In flushed slopes grows
the short-spurred fragrant orchid.
The partisans ate it
after they buried
the bodies of their friends.

Those who fled
gathered it quickly in their pockets.

If you were in a place called home,
a place of shelter and wonder

of the world, you could make
a drink or bread or jelly from the salep.

Right where the boots tread,
right where the blood seeped

the earth was trying to give you a gift.

At the Grave of a Woman Partisan, Montjuïc Cemetery, Barcelona

Does it even exist? Here is a scrabble of bones
on a special plank, draped in white cloth. Does she

have a name, and where is it kept? In the archives
of crumpled papers, mildewed, blood-stained.

Cable cars drift against the clear blue sky above
my upturned head, sun blazing my face, blinding me

for a few spotty minutes, eyes cast down at the dirt
beneath my feet. After the exhumation I dream

greyhounds race in circles in the dog park, kicking up
dust, and parakeets squabble from their huge nests.

Everything is peaceful now in this city, though the quiet
river that runs beneath the calm is deceptive, gathering

its currents into a waving flag of a nation, another victory
over the bodies of women, lost to history and walking dead

at a moment's notice. This is the whole world now, a stage
set for the corralling of bodies, to serve two purposes,

get rid of, as in *trash,* and *husband,* as in *plough.*
You must give to the regime: motherhood, pleasure,

eternal aid to powers, all else shall be discarded.
On the mountain I sift for her finger bones. Open

my notebook in the library of geography, write her name.

(   )

Teeth of heather voles

There are still so many things
I want to tell you.

A Little Golden Book of Prayer for the End of My Life

Oh God, give me the hazel
Dormouse or the garden
Dormouse, perhaps in heaven.

And I could live my whole life in the taiga
Waiting to see a flying squirrel.
Would it name me, then?
Would I just take the friendliest hand of death
And follow to the other world,
Having been so blessed?

Christmas Eve, Arles, and Goya's Bulls

You were afraid. How the cork trees broke
their spines against the wind, the crack

like a strike, lightning in the shape of antlers.
The men waved their capes in front of the bulls,

driving them deeper into darkness, bloodied
and breathless, some stunned moment that never

inhales again and all that's left is a stillborn form
of what was. I was watching over you,

I had you in my sights, ready to drag you back
to safety, some place we could name, some soil

to stick a flag into, some claim or stake. But you
just stood shell-shocked and turned around and left,

everything about us forgotten, how once
as children, we'd lie under the Christmas tree,

staring up into the lights as if the future was blessed
and brilliant, a promise, what you walked away from

what you left behind, a dead beast of hope unable
to breathe. I hope you find home. I hope

you find heaven and it flashes and flares
for you. I hope you know every delight.

The Last Place She Came Before She Took Her Own Life (This Is Not a Suicide Note)

> *"Don't be afraid—for if you can cross over, for if you have crossed, so have we all."*
> —*Fadwa Souleiman*

We found leaves like arrowheads.
We were searching for amethyst in the river's beach.

Imagine her as a girl, birds strung on a line across her chest
and the gown of mist gathering at her ankles.

It must have seemed like that like a dream so full of desire
there was just no way to hold it back. The dam broke.

You know the feeling that makes you text and text over
and over again, blocks of words in long currents of blue

and you just can't stop yourself, let yourself unravel.
You can text me like that anytime. I'll hold a place

for you at my table. Just please, *keep talking*.

So much you want to say, and it seems like no one
wants to listen. But we all *wanted* so much.

I would have listened to you. Taken all of you in.
I wish I would have.
I would make a lavalier for you,
a pendant on a frail gold chain

that held the earth of your presence.

In the aftermath I keep saying, *I'm sorry*

I keep saying, *They miss you so much.*

I'll keep saying,   *I see you*

your shadow falling over all of us,
a rustling in the treetop's cool shade.

Directions

The beech tree across from the prison doors
Has a trunk the size of an elephant now,
Bending its great head and tusks toward
The walls where the Nazis mowed down
Men and then the communists came and did.

*

What would it look like, to live without fear?
Not like us, who sleep and forget the suffering
Of those around us, riding their motorcycles
Along the dusty road, looking for fresh water.
Not us, who shut our eyes at the rising music,
Its waves of annihilation, dragging us under.

*

A woman plants geraniums in her window
And a little bit of dirt falls on the head
Of a child pulling his plastic truck by a red rope.
He does not know what has happened, doesn't see
How the people part for him, divide
Like the tsunami's first sucking tide.

First Things

The Saint wore an orange dress.
She was glowing like نارنجی in a bowl on a summer-lit table.
All around her stood columns,

smoke-blackened and bullet holes in the museum walls,
damage left since the war
as a reminder to the visitors.

I opened my mouth in awe;
I never knew they used that color orange in antiquity!
It doesn't seem old!

But then I read on the label
the color was an undercoat

and the topcoat of paint had worn away; what was once
true beauty had been damaged by time

so that this orange you see was a remnant of the *real* work.

I walked away with joy, knowing

I saw her in her nakedness and promised
to meet her again in my death,

when I walk among black columns again,
her two fingers lifted in blessing.

Terroriste

There are eight bones in your wrist. Eight stars too
in the Northern Crown in the night sky above the birches.

Yours are scattered in the dirt, coronation of some man's
headship over you. The death of every woman is a man.

I'll keep the joints from your hand, keep them *Draga*
in my purse, in my pocketbook with this pistol, engraved

with all your names. It was all worth it. Even your blood
spilled from the gash under your rib, you would still say

was all worth it. We will pour and pour like fear
from Adam's mouth. I'm a partizanka now and I hunt

with you in the thickets and through the crosshairs, turning
from slogans to murder and I have no regrets. *Propaganda*

of deeds, they said. But, what they say about revenge
is all wrong. The women who killed went on to live good

happy lives, chickens running around their heart-shaped feet,
digging their toes into the dirt, under the shade of the apple trees.

Monster

I was looking for Golem. He stood round in the middle
of the intersection, and the sirens were calling as a man's
voice echoed from the loudspeakers, ordering us where to go,
how to surrender. It was just a childhood game, you said,
a beast created by us and let loose from our own dreams,
not *real*. But here we are now, running the artery between
my body and yours, trying to escape a country suddenly at war.
Again, and again, bombardment of the same building,
reconstructed in the image of God, dismantled and rebuilt
by hands that survived raid after raid. Imagine you are an angel,
standing at the top of the radio tower and you could save us;
would you? What would you say in the waves riding the banked
clouds of transmissions: I loved you. Did you love me, too?
Would you please stop shelling and let us all go free?
The creature you made only wants to sit beside us, only wants
you to look him in the face and say, *I believe. Help my unbelief.*

The Stop

I thought there were four corpses of noblemen in the basement
of the church but there are many times more than that. I can't
remember each name and title, but I doubt they're all noble.

A woman drives my tram, #4. Her long brown hair reflects
the lights like a window at night. She peers into the dark,
careful on the curves not to hit any pedestrians or passersby.

I daydream this job is mine. But imagine what a mess
I'd make, stopping for everyone left behind, running
to catch up, as I drive on mesmerized by a rat swimming

across the pond to the left, who knows what I'd hit. Look!
His tiny paws tread water and his whiskers probe out of algae
like little antennas. O delights. O world of distraction.

I love the tram wires crisscrossing in a web from building
to building against the sky, one day storm-roiled, next day
June blue. And the people who live in their apartments,

you get to know them by sound: their cough grown deeper
in the chest, the baby's cry more frantic than before.
When the people gather at the stop, you can't tell who is who,

each gripping their ticket, each one waiting for the weather
to turn, the marriage to end, the chemo to shrink the tumor at last.
Where are we all going? An elderly woman climbs the steep steps

and we all get up to give her our seat, gasping for breath.

The Fireman's Ball

In the cinema I was the only one. It was a comedy "banned
forever" by the communists. I can never laugh at old movies,

except when the room is full and everyone else is laughing.
My flat is next door to the prison where the Nazis executed

their prisoners, shot them against the wall of the inner courtyard.
I recognized it from history. Now it's covered in art, a man

blowing bubbles from a wand, and you can see the enhanced
outline of his penis behind his tight jeans. The bubbles say,

Everyone invited! And come to the party, it's free! Let's dance!

There is a certain anticipation in every good comedy, and tension
builds to unbearable when you are alone and can't let it out.

If I'm alone in this theater in the dark, can I touch myself?
Will it make a sound?

The doctor called and said I have a rare genetic disorder, ligaments
in my neck are turning to bone, which may be the cause of my fainting.

Like a child in the childhood story showing off her scar,
I'm most proud to tell my friends, *It can cause INSTANT DEATH!*

What do the living know about anything at all? O how we love
the suspense. O how we are dying to find out what happens next.

Sleepers

I think perhaps the answer is that we should all go. The phosphorescence
of the blue beaches will glow in our absence. Do we believe the herds
of reindeer need us, won't find for themselves new paths of migration
through the desolate cities we leave behind, trampled by hooves? Felled
trees will sprout lichens and fungi, as brilliant as stars and their funnels
will siphon water to the tiny mouths of the tadpoles. New frogs will sing
I or *I am the I am* without us to listen, haunches of color and poison no one
can judge. They sing at the crossing where once the people passed, fleeing
wars, pushing their bikes on the frozen road because the law forbade walking.
Now, the snows have melted and there is singing because we have gone,
at last, we have gone. The birds nod their heads above the empty fields,
and the whale calves cleave off from their mothers, close to the shore
to say goodbye, no, to say nothing at all, only to swim freely with no
fear of us. The sea becomes one hushed lullaby for the whole, terminal
where the rubber boats tipped and drowned their desperate load, now radiant
with the reflection of stars like gold confetti, scattered in the perfect black
of night, every false idol and light burnt out. What map could chart a world,
devoid of monsters, no place *beyond*, because not one of us exists to name it.
Sea stacks stand witness, spiders nest in the seams of the earth and spin.

Unbound

Los Angeles, morning frogs and loneliness.
When I drive the 405 I feel like a god,

Getty a Greek temple on the hill above us,
bundled nurslings of clouds, artemisia I rub

between my fingers, desire's votive lit like despair
in my chest. The gods get raped, too.

Rampikes of scorched trees under the sliding mud.
Branches bird-limed to snare the wrens. No one

is safe. Look at that boy, blindfolded. Hands
tethered, Auden between his lips. I remember

the Mennonite kid smoking in the barn, smoke veiling
the features of his face, hiding out from his daddy.

I promised not to turn him in, feeling fast for the knots
he begged me to undo. Recapitulation of self

into former selves like the endless halls of mansions.
I fucked all the boys because I wanted to be them.

He said, *Me too.* Fretwork of light on his collar bone,
redwork of veins between his legs where he cut himself.

Down in the Pacific, bladderwort strewn along the beach,
and below the surface on the sea floor fauna sway gigantic

and nameless to us. We know nothing about the world. Except,
You, *rara avis* –just a glimpse of God and see me rapt now,

see me undone. I said to him: it was *you* all along who called
to me, who led me back to myself, and he said, *I tell you the God's*

honest, I had nothing to do with it. You dreamt me up,

deranged as a demon half bound by rebellion and other half
more alive than anyone I've ever known. Merwin said,

if you find you no longer believe, enlarge the temple. Believe in
Who? Who speaks for you or for me now? I never knew who

you really were, which is the true story of love.
But I was glad to see you go

one bright morning, driving past on the highway, in your glory,
bound for paradise, and I lifted my hand and waved goodbye.

Centenary

In the last air raid of the last war, a mother feeds her child.
The war ended today: the planes strafed the hills and stilled
their engines, drifting quiet over the clouds, and the gunners
stayed their fire. Flash of steel, stilled. Rain bloomed like poppies
in the fields; war's work done. Redcurrant creeps down the scarp,
berries red as blood running over the rocks and stones in heaps
where I walk, every life drawn by cell and divided. Beasts drool
to the scent of food, poison from empire's deep curse, whip
on the backs of slaves, slashing of hearts under every blade and tank.
A cut-throat God made us, tried to reap us out with flood, but we swam
on and on, said, *No,* refused to be held back from our want,
even while dying to be held at all. We wander
now, lost in this century's circuitry, fruit scattered
on the ground, dirge or ode, *feed us, feed us,* we cry out. For we are
hungry. Don't dream of the dead in their pitch and lime. Close
your eyes, try to drift closer to the ones who are gone, all the ghosts
of the un-answering-back. Be content. As if throwing violets over the wall
to a river flowing unseen, who can tell if the petals litter the bank or drift
hundreds on? Hunched against sirens and shelters of the world,
she regurgitates chewed crackers from her throat into the mouth of her infant.
In this way, hope lives. In this way, we find it is impossible not to love.

Inauguration

There were, for some of us, new weapons,
tools we found lying on the ground. Once we
came in from the garden and put away our dirty gloves
a fire blazed in the copper pots and suddenly we knew
we could kill him, a king on his throne, thick with flesh.
It was as if all along the pacifists in us had been forging
secret cells, and the message passed through us
all at once, *Every war already carries within it*
the war that will answer it   get the clubs, collect
the blades, or looking at our hands for the first time,
fingers outstretched, we realized it could be done bare-handed,
yanking by the hair, strangle his neck, or most American
of all, true to our constitution, aim the barrel for the back
of his head, the simplest thing we could manifest, a small labor
like digging up the earth and coaxing the tomatoes to grow,
like widening a pelvis to push our children into the light and arms
of a country of love. We could kill just as easily, we promised.
We sharpened our knives and now that we know,
we will never forget what it felt like.

Notes

Uxor Pilate: is the wife of Pontius Pilate, italics come from Matthew 27:19

Portrait of a Courtesan: is a painting by Caravaggio. The model, Fillide Melandroni, appeared in many of Caravaggio's paintings and was a well-known prostitute in Rome.

Demarcation Line: references the night of the Bataclan terrorist attack in Paris in November 2015. Italics are from a popular Ukrainian folk song sung during the Maidan revolution, which began November 2013.

I Want to Tell You About a Girl, Captures: title comes from the first spoken lines at the opening of the song "From Here to Eternity" by Nick Cave. The Troubles refers to the extended conflict in Northern Ireland from 1960s to the Good Friday Agreement in 1988. Line in italics is from Vladimir Nabokov. *Braucherai* is a form of Pennsylvania Dutch folk magic.

Excerpt of a Letter from the Front Line: Black Bread: Potemkin and the image of the cracked spectacles comes from the 1926 film *Battleship Potemkin* by Sergei Eisenstein.

Joan, Directors Notes: refers to the 1928 film *The Passion of Joan of Arc* by Carl Theodor Dreyer

Suffocation in Filadelfia, a Brief History of Moral Exceptions: Mennonites first settled in Eastern Ukraine in the 1700s at the invitation of Catherine the Great. There were subsequent waves of migration to Paraguay beginning in the late 1700's, with a second wave in the 1800s fleeing forced military conscription, and a third wave escaping massacre from Soviet and Nazi occupations. The Mennonites who came out of this historical context struggled with their commitment to nonresistance when faced with centuries of pogroms and terror. The early days in Paraguay were marked with disease and starvation.

Postcards from Miss World and the Angry Brigade: refers to the 1970 bombing of the Miss World event in London by the Angry Brigade, a militant left feminist organization led by Anna Mendelssohn, poet and activist.

Eye Teeth, Restraining Order: refers to the Deal barracks IRA bombing of 1989

Iftar (with the Stooges) Sarajevo: *your pretty face is going to Hell* is from the song by Iggy and the Stooges. *Man in Instant Death* is a photograph formally known as *The Falling Soldier* by Robert Capa. It is one of the most recognized war photographs of history depicting a soldier at the moment of being shot by a sniper during the Spanish Civil War. *The war is over! Long live the war!* is from Ed Vuillamy, British journalist in Bosnia during the war in the 1990s .

Kill Yr Idols, Liner Notes: title from Sonic Youth song of same name. There are also some echoes of lines and references to a photograph of Patti Smith.

Assassin in the Gallery, a Written and Signed Confession: refers to the assassination of Andrei Karlov, Russian Ambassador to Turkey, in an art gallery. The motive of the gunman is unclear but took place during protests in Turkey over Russia's involvement in the Syrian Civil War.

Bail Bond: The phrase *Terror Praesentis* in the manuscript refers to Mandelstam's "horror of the present tense." *Cooling Time* refers to the book by that title by C. D. Wright and the weird legal concept she references in which a defendant cannot use the "Heat of Passion" defense for murder if he had a long enough period of time to cool down before he committed the act. But if you didn't have enough cooling time, you might get away with it.

In the First Hour of War We Didn't believe There Would Be a War: refers to the sentiment expressed by many citizens of Sarajevo and many of my friends who endured the longest siege of any city 1992–1996. Lines in italics are from Miljenko Jergović *Sarajevo Marlboro*.

El Call: Jewish Quarter in Barcelona. Italics from a hymn, "Brightly Beams Our Father's Mercy"

Cloud of Witnesses: Lines in italics are from the film *Rosemary's Baby*.

Molotov's Announcement owes a debt of gratitude to the notebooks of Vasily Grossman, war correspondent for the Red Army beginning in 1941.

Map to the Field of Palaces: Field of Palaces comes from the name of the city Sarajevo, *saraj* for palace, *ovasi* for fields, meaning "fields around the palace" I'm not entirely sure if this is correct, but I still like it. For me the city has come to symbolize the whole terror and beauty of the world. Reference and debt of gratitude to *The Unwomanly Face of War* by Svetlana Alexievich, who documented the experiences of women partisan fighters in the USSR.
Definition of *bewilder*, Samuel Johnson, *A Dictionary of the English Language*, 1775

Cut Your Engines and Cool Your Wings: title refers to "Promised Land" by Elvis

Laying on of Hands: reference to *The Gazer Within* by Larry Levis. Last line in italics is from "Edward Hirsch: Short Conversations with Poets" by Ilya Kaminsky, *McSweeney's*, Sept 10, 2020.

Terroriste: *Draga* means *Dear* in Bosnian

The Fireman's Ball: refers to the Czech film by the same name directed by Miloš Forman

Unbound: lines in italics from W. S. Merwin "A Scale in May"

Inauguration: lines in italics are from Käthe Kollwitz

Acknowledgments

I am grateful to the editors of these publications in which these poems previously appeared, sometimes in a slightly different form or with a different title.

Cathexis Northwest, Sept. 2018, "Magnetic Girl."
Glass Poetry, Nov. 2018: "Joan, Director's Notes" first appeared as "Joan."
Gregory O'Donoghue International Poetry Competition, 2019, "Centenary."
Massachusetts Review, Volume 62, Number 1, Spring 2021, "Sleepers."
Prairie Schooner: "Suffocation in Filadelfia, a Brief History of Moral
    Exceptions."
Quarterly West, Salvage/Selvage, Issue 103, Aug. 2019: "Inauguration,"
    "Portrait of a Courtesan," and "Uxor Pilate."
Rivet, 2017, "Postcards from Miss World and the Angry Brigade."
TLR Granary, Vol. 62, Issue 02, Feb. 2020, "Eye Teeth, Restraining Order"
    first appeared as "Bite."

My deepest gratitude and love to Mary Biddinger, Amy Freels, and Thea Ledendecker; Amy Woolard, Velid Borjen Beganović, and House Martin; Tom Simpson, Alina Stefenescu, Lynne Lampe, Diane and Lon Gingerich-Feil, Steven Sams, and Adnan Kurtagić.

Heathen (Heather Derr-Smith) is a poet with four previously published books, *Each End of the World* (Main Street Rag Press, 2005), *The Bride Minaret* (University of Akron Press, 2008), *Tongue Screw* (Spark Wheel Press, 2016) and *Thrust* (Persea Books, 2017). *Outskirts* is their fifth book. Heathen is also the founder and director of Čuvaj se/Take Care, a nonprofit supporting writers in conflict zones and communities affected by trauma.